EARTH TONGUES

EARTH TONGUES

POEMS BY JOE PADDOCK

Illustrated
by
Andrew Larkin

MILKWEED EDITIONS

MINNEAPOLIS, MINNESOTA

89 88 87 86 85   5 4 3 2 1

A LAKES AND PRAIRIES AWARD BOOK
Published by *Milkweed Editions*
an imprint of Milkweed Chronicle
Post Office Box 24303
Minneapolis, Minnesota 55424
Books may be ordered from the above address

Drawings © 1985 by Andrew Larkin

Library of Congress Catalog Card Number: 85-61268
ISBN: 0-915943-07-7

ACKNOWLEDGEMENTS

"Kingsryder and McGraw" was originally published in *Preview* magazine; "Johnny Horseapple" in *The Roadapple Review*; "Black Energy," "Between Tigers," and "Leaf Dance, Life Dance" in *Milkweed Chronicle*, "Frogs" in *The Journal of Fresh Water* and *The Lake Street Review*; and "Waiting for Spring" in *North Country Anvil* and *Twenty-five Minnesota Poets #1*. Several other poems in this collection were published by projects with which I have worked, but have never been distributed to a general literary audience.

Within "Prairie Waters" and "The Lead Wagon" there are short quotes from oral history. These have been printed in italics. I collected and edited this material myself, and it was originally published in *The things We Know Best*. My thanks to Book 200, Inc. of Olivia, Minnesota, for permission to reprint it here.

My thanks, too, to Laurence Stadther of Olivia, Minnesota, who originally told me the stories from which "The Meeting" and "First Goddess" were developed. I should mention that Laurence is not the old man remembering in "First Goddess." Thanks also to Delmar Debbaut for the story that became "Frogs."

To the Memory of My
Mother and Father

CONTENTS

I

II

III

IV

I

PRAIRIE WATERS

A billion years of rain,
and then the snow and the hail fell
over what was
to become these prairies. Then
within warm bays, swollen
with time, a new rain,
too fine for the naked
human eye — had there been such —
invisible rain   of life   born from
that water, and
in the joy and joke of time, this life
took a long slow leap into   lizards
which dwarfed strange trees.

Then a great, patient pendulum
of ice,   glaciers,
marking time   and life   possibilities,
came and went and left great lumps in moraine
which became bright lakes,
and inland seas of melt-water leaned
against melting southern faces, and deep
underground bodies of water began to drift
through porous earth.

And how many scores of millions of years
of migrations,   winging
north   and again south? Ducks and geese,
swans, cormorants, cranes
climbing the air, riding wind, awesome
body of migration, its flyway of throats
crying love
of sky and that water which winked
and flashed beneath, which teemed
with fish and otter, beaver and mink,
the fine unseen rain.

Then for just a wing-beat
of time, men and women,
Indians and then whites, cradling in skulls
a gray mass of change,
bellied down to creeks and drank water
sweet and clean as the scent
of the prairie rose, listened
to chuckle and slap
of waves against rich shores.
Men and women saw their faces, souls
mirrored,   miracle
of still water.

Then,
about one lifetime back,
water was too abundant.
Man and woman couldn't travel
in a straight line.
Couldn't grow crops
everywhere.   Old Fred remembered
first ditches:
Went in around '12 or '14.
I was a kid. Those big dippers —
They'd float 'em, and they'd drop the scoop
on the ground, and pull themselves forward.
We kids, we'd go down and ride on it.
I tell you, that was somethin'
when the big ditch come through.

Ever'thing is tiled out now.
My home place out there,
what my dad bought, there was a big slough
on the northwest corner,
and one on the southwest.
That was one hundred and sixty acres,
but could only farm about a hundred.
Now, that's all drained out, farmed
one end to the other.

The potholes are gone.
The potholes are gone!
All but one
for every thousand
that once laughed cattails
in the wind.

Whole lakes!
Whole lakes are gone:
Swan and Butler, Berry and Brandt
no longer exchange
glitter and flash for primal
cries of great
migrations   waning
in Autumn skies.

Wet year and dry   tile
drinks the rain and runs it clean
to straightened creeks.
And woe to the man or woman
who bellies down
and drinks deep of that water.
If the poison doesn't get them,
the fertilizer will.

Still, the corn grows tall,
the cornfields roll
in an endless flood
of green,   lapping the air,
but the water's gone bad   or gone
for good: pothole, lake,
even the deep unimaginable
underground sea, Ogallala,
beneath the circles, the turning
center-pivot irrigators, reaching
from Dakota to Amarillo,
now shrinks and burns, bad
for the fine rain
of life   and light
in the eyes of child, gosling, heifer,
last buffalo.

Lost in the backwaters
of a nursing home,
old Fred's voice flows on:
How long did it take
to get this area drained? Well,
they're still draining.
By gol, you know, even this last summer
there was just a lot of tile put in.
Oh, I tell you, this country has changed.
Sometimes I think things
is goin' too fast.
Somethin' is goin' to break
some of these days.

Voice calm
in a town with corn
lapping, lapping
at its every shore.

THE MEETING

Two women past the noon
of their lonely lives,
before the turn
of our century,   met weekly
under a circling hawk on a hilltop between
their farm homes on the bleak
Minnesota prairie.

There was no other woman for miles.

One spoke Norwegian, the other Bohemian.
A black and white dog lay between them,
sometimes whimpering as they tried,
across prairies of difference,
with smiles and intense light
from their eyes,
to exchange small particular things
from their lives:
> *picking cabbage worms and potato bugs,*
> *stripping feathers for ticks,*
> *nursing children, churning butter, darning socks,*
> *starting barrels of kraut, boiling fat for soap,*
> *catching a pitcher of blood from the cut throat*
> *of a hog. . . .*

Small particulars,
froth from the surface
of inner rivers   dammed
through silent days,
loosed now in the movement of hands,
hungering in air.

They chuckled and clucked, but could not quite
loosen their bodies
to dance their lives
for each other.

And the black and white dog whined
as if something in his brain too knew
of an immense effort toward speech.

The two women then said their different goodbyes,
till the next week.
A strong formal handshake,
and the hawk-swept sky,
as they strode back through tall grass
to their homes and their men,
was luminous again.

FIRST GODDESS

Ah, the naked bodies
of those two girls.
Even now . . . .
But that was seventy years back.
"It was the stiffest lickin'
I ever got," said Ernest.
The shifting winds of memory played
in his face and eyes
like sunlight and shadow over prairie grass.

They swam naked in that tiny pond.
Spring fed. Cattails ringed it.
A lone upthrust willow stood at its western edge.
The Hellman girls, Bonnie and Nora,
swam naked there
in the deep heat of July
when even the prairie did not breathe.
Rode the three miles from their farm home,
double, on a lively gray gelding.
Stripped dresses and blouses from their sweaty skins,
splashed in
with shouts and groans of delight,
quenched their bodies
in the cool water of that pond.

And old Ernest, barely eleven then,
came upon them and quickly
dropped to his belly
in the tall sweet grass of that virgin prairie,
and wormed slowly over the swelling   earth
till he lay close to that female joy.
"I was just learnin' to see
the whys and wherefores of a woman's body,"
said Ernest, "and they was worth a look,
the pair of 'em. Supple and lean, with breasts
like a Holstein. Known to be bold, you know."

There under the great heat
of the July sun, the prairie grass waved and swayed
before Ernest's eyes which
drank the full breasts and shocking white flesh
of the Hellman girls.
They splashed and shrieked while,
in the single upthrust willow,
a redwing blackbird (they were too near its nest)
scolded them
and sometimes sang.

Then, a desire, a hunger for power or play,
stirred in Ernest.
He must do something
to prove mastery of the situation.
"Their clothes was layin' there,
all piled neat. I thought
I'd 'Injun' in without their knowin'.
Carry them around to the far side of the hill.
Then wait and see."

Ernest edged in, and the girls,
their bare white rumps sometimes flashing in the sun
as they somersaulted in water,
did not see him. Ernest touched
the very cattails, but he had not counted
upon the pond's guardian ring of frogs.
As he passed, one sprang, *pock*!
into the water, and a chain
of others followed on around the pond.
The gray gelding, tethered to the willow,
neighed and threw his head.
Nora, the older, glided up from water,
stood at the pond's edge, one-footed, neck stretched,
white and poised as an egret
about to strike a fish.

Young Ernest, his heart leaping like the frogs,
was up and running, legs pumping,
his feet tangling in tough
prairie grass. He stumbled and fell,
glanced back to see
long-haired Nora, a switch in her hand,
running from the pond
to the gray gelding.
Breath burning in his lungs, Ernest
was up again and running, the great prairie whirling
about him, and again he glanced back to see
that naked young woman, her long hair streaming,
sailing down upon him like a prairie falcon.

She leapt
from horseback to his back.
"Ooof!" said Ernest. "I was flattened.
Left my wind
in the roses."
The smell of the swamp was on her.
He remembers yet
the rich crush of breast across his face
as Nora wrestled him around
and lashed his behind
with her switch.

Ernest succumbed
to that sweet naked beating.
As he spoke of it, all these seventy years later,
something still shined out
from the shallows of his watery eyes.
He spoke in perfect mime
of Nora: "Ernie, you little bastard!"
She gripped his ears in her fists,
shook his head from side to side.
Then she was up, was riding away.

Ernest lay there in the grass,
fingers gripping down into roots,
sometimes giggling, with tears searing
his eyes and cheeks.
Something immense was swelling in his chest.
He stood soundlessly shaking clenched fists,
and deep at the core of his brain
the gray gelding, complete again,
rose powerfully on his hind legs
and loosed a shriek
which ripped the entire prairie sky
to shreds.

THE LEAD WAGON

Together, the whole
neighborhood rode, rocking,
in the lead wagon.
Neighbors talking, blackbirds
flocking, turned as one,
sang in the cattails
in the living marshes
the wagons wound around
on their slow and easy way
to town.

Those farmers around Roseland
had no railroad, had to come to Danube.
Three hour drive with a load.
Couldn't trot your horses
on those old dirt roads
with a load of grain
or livestock.

Two tracks
in heavy black dirt.

Some of the richest land in the world,
those Renville County roads.

Slow, slow, threading complexity:
three creeks, half the ground low,
vast cattail swamps.
The ditcher and dozer
had only just begun
their plunge   into earth.

Depot agent.
I had a good view north.
Could watch 'em comin' in.
Regular wagon train.
Each family had their own,
but they'd all be settin' together
on the lead wagon.
The horses took care
of the haulin'.
Whether they tied the hitchin' straps
to the end-gate rods,
or whether they just naturally followed,
I don't know,
but that's the way they come in,
havin' a party
in the lead wagon.

Slow, slow, over gumbo black land
which fed wheat and potatoes, fed
bone and the surging
of that neighborhood's blood, fed
sudden flock-flights
of words   over quiet
of prairie, that great leap
of sky.   Creaking
of wagons. Steady walking clop
of Percherons and Belgians.
Thin line of geese   meeting
jack rabbits bouncing
high into the horizon.

A harmonica, a song.

Blackbirds, rising,
turn as one.

KINGSRYDER AND MCGRAW

This all began
with our great grandfathers.
They saw.
They actually saw this rolling prairie
without a fence,   antelope and buffalo,
before the plow
turned it all over, and now . . . .

They *saw* the great migrations which began
aeons before Man ever dreamed
God!
And now
half that soil, that top stuff, heaven of roots,
created in the joy
and agony, the birth and death of every
June bug, jack rabbit, coyote . . . .
life churning through itself,   dark and bloody,
lovely ground . . . .

And now
it is half gone, swift as passenger pigeons,
down
drainage ditches, channeled rivers,
through clean farms to the Mississippi,
to some gulf,
this prairie:
vast, sad motherhump
in the throat of our river.

I didn't see the unfenced prairies,
the buffalo   and the passenger pigeon
go out like fires,
but remember men who did,
or who were close enough
to tell the tale in the way they lived,
violent old men,
filled with hellish fun.

There were Kingsryder and McGraw.
Back then
McGraw ran the coffee shop.
Kingsryder was an old man
who dressed each day in a black suit
and black, high-topped old man's shoes,
and carried a cane for the power that was in it.

>Back then
>it seemed that all of this had gone on forever,
>but these prairies had only just been turned.
>This was our first generation of old men,
>violent as old bull buffalo on their knees, bubbling
>their last blood.

Each day at three in the afternoon, Kingsryder,
entering the coffee shop, all bustle and self-importance
around some emptiness within, I suppose,
>or maybe just that storm
>of hellish fun,
would whack his cane on the counter
for attention,
call for donuts and coffee,
begin his noisy complaint, dead pan:
"Goddamn, McGraw, you got an old bull
'round back what craps these donuts?"
Then lifts his cup: "McGraw,
whose radiator'd you drain today?"

>These two men over many years had never once
>   embraced.
>Never once had thrown a friendly arm around
>the other's shoulder.
>Perhaps, even, never once shaken hands.

And McGraw, over the years, always irritated,
would only say, "Goddammit, Kingsryder, one of these days
I'm gonna shoot you!"
And *whack!* goes the cane across a counter that
not twenty years back had been an oak
on the Darwin Prairie.

"Draw your weapon, McGraw! Play your hand!"

And so McGraw sent away somewhere
for a box of blanks
for his old hog-leg revolver,
and comes the day – there's a half-dozen coffee soaks
there – when Kingsryder asks:
"McGraw, you got a deal with old Moon Beckstrand
what cleans the streets?"
And McGraw says, deadly between his teeth:
"Kingsryder, I've told you!"
Then he reaches slow under the counter,
comes up with his revolver,
and the place is so still
that you can hear
a crow cawing for something lost
way off at the edge of town.
Kingsryder's cane wavers. Not a snake-tongue flicker,
but a waver,   like the antenna
of a confused insect.

> How does an old Indian fighter die,
> when, in fact, he'd never really . . . ?

McGraw's face is cold.
KA-BAM! goes the piece.
Kingsryder's eyes show white in a faint,
and he slides from his stool to the floor,
and the six coffee-drinkers pass through the door
    like whippets,
shouting:
"MCGRAW SHOT KINGSRYDER!
        MCGRAW SHOT KINGSRYDER!"

We laughed about it for years. It tuned up our lives,
and emptied Kingsryder of half his style.
Who's to say the fright didn't knock a bit
    from the tail end of Kingsryder's days?
Or who's to say Kingsryder's insults hadn't done
    as much for McGraw?

They're both gone now.
They were our first generation of old men,
violent as old bull buffalo on their knees, bubbling
their last blood.

They knew a great, mad moment
of a sort of health,
but their passing
is a healing. I, we,
began about here.

OLD MARTIN

His name was Martin, Old Martin,
and he was bent in the back,
nearly double, and a great hump,
under his blue work shirt, rode him
like a buzzard.

For years, in the background
of the dust-filled memory of our town,
he'd swung
hundred pound sacks of feed
onto trucks and into boxcars.

Work was his passion.
He honed his love and his hate
against work,
and grew lean and folded into himself
like a jackknife.

In Garner's Pool Hall,
I listened while a man
whose belly rolled over his belt
like a dead goose
sipped a beer and said,
"Ol' Martin's all bent over like that
because he lost a quarter
when he was a small boy,
and he's been lookin' for it
ever since."

WHEN OLD MEN WATCHED TRAINS

I remember how,
when I was a boy, old men with canes
strolled into that park
alongside the tracks   in the twilight,
and a trembling in the earth began.

A trembling in the earth,
then a rumble,
and that first distant blaring of horn.

    It would have been
    somewhere east of Darwin then,
    rocketing out of those hardwood hills.
    And young deer lifted their heads from clover
    and listened.

And those old men,
leaning on their canes, knew
that a train
was somehow a life,
hurtling out of nowhere
and vanishing into the vast.

And for those few moments
of actual, immense presence,
when the train thundered past
and the earth billowed
and their flesh shuddered around their bones,
they were, by God, *alive!*
and they waved their canes,
maybe at grim death,
as the train hurtled west.

    O, Santa Fe all the Way!
    Orange Blossom Special!
    The Way of the Zephyrs!

And after a time,
the old men stood spent
in the green silence of that park,
and the singing of robins grew large again
in the near-night air.

FROGS

At that time there was still a pothole
over every hill, and the frogs in the fall
swarmed like maggots in the carcass of a dead horse.
Sometimes, after the coming of the cars,
they had to get out the blade to scrape the slick
of crushed frogs off that road that circles
    Stork Lake.

One sunny Saturday afternoon in late September,
more than forty years back now,
down around the bay,
about fifteen town kids began to herd frogs
up from the water's edge where they lay
dozing in the sun by the thousands,
big heavy leopard frogs that would stretch
nine, ten inches from nose to toe claw.

They herded them slowly
up over Anderson's pasture hill.
You would've thought it was wind through grass
sweeping ahead of them.
Herded them up onto the road into town,
herded them with real care, losing a few here
    and there,
but maintaining the mass
(some guessed five thousand, some ten),
and at the corner of Sixth,
they turned them, losing maybe forty dozen
which bounced on over Hershey's lawn,
confusing the beJesus out of their old basset
    hound, Monty,
who, after sniffing and poking with his paw,
sat down and howled at a thin silver sliver
    of day moon
in the sky.

Old Mrs. Angier said she first heard a sound
like five thousand hands patting meat,
and when she looked up the street, she saw
these kids, serious and quiet, with a grey-brown wave,
like swamp water to their knees,
rolling along in front of them.

Mrs. Angier said, "Now, you never heard a word
from a single one of those kids.
They were silent and strange with that haze of a wave
rolling along in front of them.
Just that patting sound
times five thousand.
I tell you, it made the goose flesh roll
up my back and arms!"

The boys claimed later that they had no plan,
but, when they came alongside "Horse" Nelson's
Fixit Quick Garage — which contained
maybe a half-dozen broken-down cars
and "Horse" and Allen, his son, and "Windy" Jeffers —
one kid barked: "Bring 'em on in!"
And they turned that herd of frogs on a dime
(they were herding easy by this time),
and ran them through the entranceway.
Young Jim Hedeen grabbed the handle
of the sliding door and rolled her shut,
and those kids vanished like fifteen rabbits
into whatever weed patch they could find.

Well, hell, you can imagine.
"Windy" was on his back working upward on a spring
when those slimy devils started sliding all over him.
They say he most-near tipped that Model A on its side
getting out of there. And "Horse,"
who was no doubt nearly through his daily pint
of peach brandy, dropped a cam shaft
on Allen's toe and ran and hid in the can,
and Allen, who'd been mean and noisy
from his first squawk on, began hopping one-footed
amidst that froth of frogs. (And you *know*

how they have a way of climbing
up the inside of your pants, all wet
and with those scratchy little claws!)
Allen, slam-banging whatever came to hand,
tipped a couple cars from jacks and screamed:
"I'M GONNA GET KEVIN KLIMSTRA FOR THIS!"

Forty-three years have passed,
but those frogs have never quit rolling
from the tongues of people around town.
It's one of those stories you learn early
and carry with you, and measure
the taste of life by
till the day you die.

II

EARTH TONGUES

This seething earth
everywhere writhes up
into tongues
of life, each telling
a perfect story
which ends in death
again   and again
and again . . . .

FISH CLEANING

I was six or eight or ten,
and those fish were the first fish
ever caught,
and those lakes were the deep lake
in my mind.
And in the deep night
in an island of light, within
the old garage,
a swirling heaven of moths,
Dad and Harry and I cleaned the fish,
and a deep rich tiredness
grew in my bones,
while the voices I loved best droned
and chuckled over the catch:
great panfish, crappies and bluegills,
that made a canepole crackle.
And those fish shivered and slapped
on that green wooden box.

We scraped slime, guts, and golden
fish eggs, still-gasping severed heads,
and a rainbow mush of scales,
slosh! into the bucket,
all to be planted still
that night beneath the roots
of our garden.

And within my weary laden mind,
dragonflies still skipped from bobber to line to pole tip.
And the bobber, red and white, quivered and slipped
down through clear water,
down into a darkness
of greater fish.

I was six or eight or ten,
and those fish were the first fish
ever caught,
and the voices of those men
were the voices I loved most,
and their drone contained me
while moths tap-tapped against
the bright burning
of their love,
and I slipped slowly, slowly down
into that dark lake
in my mind.

THE WEAK LIGHT

There is sadness in the weak light
of November, its late afternoons.
Fields plowed black and vacant.
The planet tipped, the angle leaves
too little heat,
and we hunch around the embers
left at our center.
Our breath escapes   as visible vapor,
vanishes   so quickly,
like that life that was summer.
And now
just that hint of sun
along the rim
of earth.
We reach an open hand
toward what has been
for so many months   generous.
Receive only
cool emptiness.

THE GEESE

A long line of geese wavers
across bright sky, calling,
and without a single thought,
white faces
of men and women
turn upward to them,
and each, lost in flight,
is a child again,
and within each mind,
a still pond opens
where the geese will settle
for the night.

LOVE SOIL

Love soil, soil love,
dusty soil, gravel soil, mellow . . . .
Weed strewn, weed seed, sparrow feed, brush . . . .
Open field edging oak,
tractor tread cow flop, soil-shit-love.
Creatureprints, fox deer pheasantprints, mice.
Net and web,   intersections.
Imprinted,
penetrated,
flesh-eating love soil.
Sinking sick into under,
sprouting back
differently the same.

BLACK ENERGY

Life is seething in this soil
which has been millions of years
in the making.
It has been forever
in the making.

A mingling of everything
which ever whistled here, leaped
or waved in the wind.
Plants and animals,
grasses of this prairie.
Buffalo and antelope grazing down
into roots   and back again
into the sun.
Birds and insects, their wings still hum
in this soil.

And this swarm drinks
sunlight and rain,
and rises again   and again
into corn and beans
and flesh and bone.

The quick bodies of animals and men
risen
from this black energy.

MEADOWLARK

Over the brown grass of early spring
the songs of meadowlarks
hurt my bones
with their sweetness.

I am a yes
to that song.
If I had one such true utterance,
I would repeat it at intervals
through every day of my life.

CONTINUANCE

The days of his life
and all they contained:
    spring moon over apple blossoms,
    gutted deer and bumper crops
    of wheat, a young wife's thighs
    shriveling in time
    like windfalls . . . .

These days streamed
through his body and mind,
all those many years,
and when they heaved
his ashes into the wind,
all over the world, rivers
of seasons
continued to murmur:
apple blossoms, deer, wheat, wife . . . .

And he was in them.

III

CARP

Carp came with us,
and we are one,
a pretty good metaphor,
one for the other. Carp's
a mirror to our way.

"It's the goddamn carp!
Muddy the water, ruin
the fishing, suckin'
up the spawn. Root
out the rice beds, rushes. Ducks
have shifted flyways, east and west . . . ."

We bring ourselves
and our bodies are more
than our bodies. That German angler
hooked by the heavy run of bronze,
big-scaled body. That power
had become him, and he longed into
larger currents: a tank of carp blown
over the ocean — most fertile,
fastest-growing fish . . . . The carp,
stops the pyramid:
bottom hog, transforms mud-rich first flowerings
    of life
to carp flesh.
Inevitably, now, everywhere here,
across all bottoms — lakes, streams, swamps —
pushed by powerful carp
hunger for life,   that replicating body
by the billion. The spawn even
riding the wind,   caught
on feathers of duck and goose,
coot and tern.

See
that cloud of mud, churned
from the bottoms by the body
of carp. Changing everything. This one
introduction and
entire ecosystems   must shift
and again shift   and again . . . .
The kaleidoscope is poor
expression of infinite
adjustments following upon the carp mouth
dredging the bottoms of our waters
everywhere, now, carp sucks, smacks
its lips against sunken logs,
rush, root,   digests,
manures the bottom.

Four years old, I heard
fish flesh hit, *whap!*
the still surface,   saw
rings roll outward,   saw
Jim swing his worm-baited bamboo rig
to the center and, uncharacteristically,
carp sucked it down, and that pole crackled
to my immense four-year-old lake
of delight.   He landed it. Strange
to hear   that carp was
"No good."
Contemptuous faces (though somehow excited).
Not food for *us*. We threw
carp over the chicken fence. Big
scales, the eyes dulled
as it flopped in dust. "Tastes
good as worms. To chickens."
I watched through mesh
harsh beaks,   swift,   greedy
as bottom-feeding carp   opened
a meaty side,   drew
pink strings of gut
into the light. An image
blossomed: arthritic
grandmother hands in skeins

of yarn, knitting
into the tissue
of our small flock of chickens:
food for us.

"Your carp is no good
to eat. Except I got
one recipe that works. You take
a three-pound carp and bake
him slow, two hours
on a cedar shingle
with a mixture
of soy sauce and ginger.
When it's done
so the meat is falling
from the bones,
you throw away the carp
and eat the shingle."

Warm summer days, kids, we rowed
leaky duck boats over
lily pad mud bays
where the heavy, powerful
bodies of carp moved through
clarity   easier
than pelicans through air. Could
not be caught, even approached.
Sudden releases   of the primal
energy,   great accelerations   soft
clouds of mud rose
to our awe,   and we would stop,
consciousness rocking gently,
in contemplation   over
the perfection of lily on water,
jewel risen   from the awesome   root
which groped muck – the power
of carp bottoms.

Like sin
we struggle to eliminate   carp
from our shadow
deeps.   Traps
built of thin slats across
the inlets of our lakes
to catch the spawning run
of carp in spring,   eliminate
that swelling and pernicious
hungry flesh . . . .

"That trap between Stella and Washington?
By God! you could walk on their backs.
Like pigs, their backs, that thick. Got
to be forty-pounders in there."

Carp came with us,
and we are one, and good metaphors,
one for the other. We are to the land
as carp to the water:
rooting,   breeding,   turning
everything over. Have sunk ourselves even
into flesh of carp:

"Up Sucker Creek, I got a spear into
the heaviest carp I ever seen!
Stronger than me. Hell,
I had him   half
up the bank, flopping . . . . He bent
the tines and wrestled free.
A big wave just   surged
between those banks . . . ."

"Gotta shoot low
with a bow or .22. Refraction.
Hit him and he'll make
a blood-run wave
like a lung-shot buck. Or
he might just rise
to the surface, turn
on his side."

Whatever such violence   means
in our minds,   our lives,
the body of carp   absorbs it
like the mud from which it rises
and thrives.

"The Department of Natural Resources took
fifty tons from Little Jim.
S'posed to be all
gone. Hell, next
year you couldn't tell
the difference."

"They don't want
to clean them out. Never keep a fish
smaller than your forearm.
Eliminate the carp,
and they'd eliminate
their jobs. They sell
carp for money
to damn fools out east
for pink salmon."

Pink salmon, smoked carp, fertilizer
for the fields.

"The best damn fertilizer you could ever
ask for. Hell, Hugo took all
he could get one year. Stink!
Lord, for stink, but you shoulda saw
the crop! Hunnert an' ten bushel corn
back before the hybrids
and anhydrous."

Feeding food for *our* flesh.
Our fertile prairie   eroded
till the lakes turned shallow. Much
has become carp flesh. Fertilizer fish
wholesome   to its own
ground. A good
circle. The body of carp
brought back – flesh, fish emulsion –
returned to roots, that we might eat
carp crops   may
be more –   The Orient

flies the flag of carp.
Grandfather carp: slow, whiskered,
the perfect movement
of Tao   now and again grasped
in glintings of sunlight from scales
in tanks, rice paddies,
floating up from dark mud
bottoms of the mind. Flesh-word
risen from nothingness, the primordial
unconscious, and into, too,
the human belly
of the Orient: carp
has fed more
human flesh   than all other fish, and
as the century takes its turn,
we, too, may have our turn
at picking fat flesh from that thicket
of forked bones, by-passing
the chicken, and eating the words
"No good!" Glad,
by God and Gaia! after all
that carp – mirror to ourselves –
came with us, and
we are one.

IV

FAUST AGAIN

"I see an angel hovers o'er thy head,
And with a vial full of precious grace . . . ."

Chistopher Marlowe, *Dr. Faustus*

Their moccasins gentle on endless prairies,
the Mother's body,   her sacredness.
They would not cut her hair to feed
their horses,   take from her the gentle loving
of a horse's muzzle,
the nip and pull.

But immigrant dreaming
of wealth and power was willing
to gut his mother for a vein
of copper
or a nickel.

Power was given the heartless practical.
(Was there a bargain?)
        U S A arrived,   1958,   first totally profane
        society   in human history.
        I am not saying evil. I am saying all
        that was sacred
        had been discounted,
        and so: chemicals,   instruments, $$$ . . . .

The Mother skinned alive.
Top foot of buffalo prairie turned
human flesh.

Buffalo within remaining sod
swell at the temples,   paw.
(Hear the rumble?)
The bargained-for four-and-twenty years
have passed.
Devil's rich laughter,
his reaching hand.

Is this hell?

AS I PASSED

As I passed,
a fox squirrel leapt from grass
to the trunk of a dying elm,
circled cautiously, watching me.
Nothing exposed, but a nose,
bright eyes, and points of ears.

Inside the house—
closed doors, closed windows—
a hound, alone, bellowed.
Such ears! To hear
the soft sound of my sandaled feet
as I passed.
A hound alone
in a box of a house
bellowed to himself.

Further along, the parked cattle truck
heaved and groaned
as the weight of its load
shifted over springs.
I could hear the breathing,
the clunk of hooves on planks,
soft bellows and moans.
Through slats, dozens
of heavy-boned legs
shifting, shifting.
The swing and swish of tails,
and as my eyes widened with the dark,
they saw eyes peering back
through slats. Soft, dark eyes which caught
tiny glintings of light,
answering my curiosity
without hostility,
staring at me
as I passed.

WAITING FOR SPRING

Out-talking geese,
but making less sense,
we migrate constantly
to winter.

That springtime of nights:
goose-gabble moonlight blend
over prairie,
the flocks riding
thousands of miles of wind
as ice drifts north.

Walking alone on moonlit prairie,
goose talk falling through the night
like spring snow:
     ankle deep in goose joy,
     I'm filled with love,
     but can't fly.

Ah, the geese,
at home in the wind,
the marshes, the seasons.

Who am I? Who are we?
What are we to do?

THE HIVE

After first snow,
in a clearing in the woods,
I came upon bee hives wrapped in black
plastic sheeting
for the winter,
and over the sheeting
an even sprinkling   of bodies:
fuzzy and frozen   honeybees.

Had gone out too far, stayed away too long,
lured perhaps by gene-implanted dreams
of that flower which precedes
flowers,   its deep glow
luring these determined bees
outwards. (O, I layered my life over
those frozen bits.) But,
that flower, one sip of such sweetness
would pay   for all
anguishing distance between
them and the shimmering
body of the hive.

On their return, who knows what gained
while cold and alone, what sip
of nectar carried
back for queen,
hive and drone, thousands of plodding workers,
to find black plastic wrapping between
them and what had become   their desire,
their home, somewhere down within,
heated through the cold winter by the hum
(*they could feel it as they froze!*)
of a hundred thousand wings
around a golden cone
of sweetness, all
a single droning body   which dreamed not
of the flower   because it was
the flower.

THE SPRING I TRAPPED
PREGNANT RACCOONS

Spring of '68.
Camped above pastures and the lake.
Meadowlarks sang through days,
through moonlit nights.

Raccoons.
Someone wanted to peer
into their blood
while they were round
with young.

Why did my eyes
ache to cry?

Painful prairie beauty.
I was broke,   sick,   losing.
My scientist drove too sharp —
Rigged with needles,
          tranquilizers
          (animals slobbering, quivering, snoring).
Below in the old man's chicken shack,
caged bulging females,   turning . . . .

The geese came through that spring
like they hadn't for forty years.
Lakes,   ponds,   spring cornfields rang,
and wingbeat goose laughter rattled
my cage of fright.

Leaving at daylight hopeless old Ford sick
my throat   I couldn't swallow
while buffalograss countryside rippled laughter.

Trapping anything   swollen
with new spring:
skunks, muskrats, mink,
beaver, fox, squirrels,   raccoons, raccoons . . . .
Such death in me!
Those animals fought to be free!
Bit my fingers,
chewed away their teeth
against steel mesh. They killed themselves!

O, long moonlit nights of meadowlarks.
Skies of goose joy.
My thin cage of sleep containing
my thousand frightened animals,   turning,
straining bone slats,   sinew wraps.
Tendons snapping.
The heart hurts
night after night.

And then I woke.   I woke.
I woke dissolving.
Climbed the grassy bluff in the dark.
I was dissolving.
All that my mind gripped around
                dissolving.

Finished and in tears
I took into me
blue lake,   a mist in tatters
bird song,   dew,
streaks of dawn.

I swelled
over and over again
with the life
of an entire spring.
Released
the bulging female
from this cage of bone.

DECOY

Decoy,
afloat on my shelf of books —
paint chipped away, blasted with shot —
your power is still good.
I swim in your wake
of memories.

You were one of those, decoy,
there were seven,
carved solid from pine. (Those roots lived
in deep silences.)
I, hip-booted, hauled in a gunny sack,
far out into the marsh
in pre-dawn blackness,   entangling
in mists of forever,
and above, invisible, wings whistling,
the morning's first flights of ducks.

Decoy,
you floated with your flock
in a half-moon   with amoral eyes of glass,
and your power was good,   brought great
energy down
to where I crouched
in cattails.
Your power was good   and fed
migrations and the sky
into my veins.

Those ducks, decoy,
those mallards,   bluebills,   teal
did not, I think, simply
mistake you for their kind.
No, you pull deep
from that center
where we quiver
everywhere together   magic:
the carving controls the species.

That vision is lost,   and its song.
That vision . . . lost . . . .

No!
no, decoy,
your power is *still* good.
You rock again gently within
waves of this shelf,
everywhere connected.
Your magic
in mind,   every wingbeat ever,
thrumming
in the wind.

BETWEEN TIGERS

(from a Zen story)

A tiger above,
a tiger below:

    sometimes nibbling needle teeth
    of cancer,

    sometimes hurtling tons
    of metal.

And we hang
on a vine
on the face of the cliff,

a tiger above,
a tiger below:

    sometimes sudden
    great pressure in the chest,

    sometimes the impudent razor
    of a stranger
    who wants . . . .

And a black mouse
and a white mouse
(always and everywhere)
have begun
to nibble on the vine,
but, in the midst,
with our noses to the rough
granite wall,
within arm's reach,
a seam where dirt in the winds of eternity
has bedded for a bit,
and up from it   green
small circular serrated leaves,

thin stems,   celebratory dance
of the strawberry plant,
and one dead ripe

  (as if
  a single clot of gore
  from the lungs
  of a shot buck)

strawberry.

A tiger above,
a tiger below.

The hand reaches out, plucks,
brings berry to mouth.
It becomes one
with the tongue.

It tastes so sweet!

JOHNNY HORSEAPPLE

Found!
my mission:
sack of steaming horse turds
under my arm,   wander
chemical country,   the Midwest,
pitching:

one here,   one there,
one here,   one there . . . .

And old earth sucks 'em down.
She's gone skinny
on bad medicine.
Listen to her groan
for pure pleasure.

One here,   one there,
one here,   one there . . . .

Moist from the fingers,
handfuls of the true,   till:

> *"Found!   Horseshit in*
> *fat of polar bear,*
> *high arctic!"*

Mother-lovin' gleam in my eye.

Tales,   songs
written in dust
(till green again)
of the wandering
horseapple man.

LEAF DANCE, LIFE DANCE

Oak leaves, walnut, willow and ash . . . .
I rake and haul, heave barrel after barrel
onto the fenced-in compost heap, till full
for the tenth time, and I toss my beagle over
the fence, climb the little ladder and leap after,
and we dance the pile down.

This is what we live for.
We stomp and leap and roll,
and Ring's sometimes almost altogether
gone, as he sounds after something which stinks
(dead sparrow or tire-smashed squirrel),
just the whipping white tip of his tail
which I sometimes grip till he flounders
to the surface, his eyes filled
with immense light. *"Down there!*
Down there!" Every writhing nuance
of his body speaks: *"Down there!"*

So much life *must* love death,
its smell and promise. Up and down!
Up and down! We leap and roll and dance,
smashing dead
leaves down tighter and tighter in the pile.

And even now
a new dance begins which will flame
high in spring,
when I mix in manure and the sun
leans near, and insects, worms
and forty billion bacteria to some incredible power
swarm in this ton of leaves. Up and down!
Up and down! Leap and dance! Snarl and eat!
Die in again
for sheer joy!

Joe Paddock lives in Litchfield, Minnesota with his wife Nancy. He is the author of *Handful of Thunder: A Prairie Cycle* (Anvil Press, 1983), and has published a book of oral history, *The Things We Know Best*. In 1975, he began a series of rural arts and humanities residencies, including: Writer in Residence for Lakewood Community College in White Bear Lake, Minnesota; Regional Poet for the Southwest Minnesota Arts and Humanities Council; Poet in Residence for Minnesota Public Radio (at Worthington); and Humanist in Residence for the American Farm Project of the National Farmers Union. He is currently a humanities consultant with the St. Paul based Land Stewardship Project. He has published frequently in magazines and journals, and is the author of two chapbooks, *Stored Light*, and *A Song Like My Own*. His work grows out of a deep personal understanding of the environment he writes of.